ESSSENCE OF ALL RELIGIONS

NILESH KUMAR AGARWAL

This book 'The essence of all religions' is dedicated to all those people who give equal respect to all religions. Those who have been created by God, believe in this world that God resides somewhere in every human being. This book will act as a guide for all those who have not learned to respect all religions in their life. I hope that this book will be helpful to some extent in improving everyone's mindset and questions regarding different religions of the people.

Thank you!

Contents

Preface

When a human is born into this world, he does not know anything. Whatever his parents, relatives, friends, teachers, etc. teach him, that knowledge gives him the direction to live life. But how much of that knowledge is right and how much is wrong, how can it be decided? It is decided by the scriptures composed by God. It doesn't matter which religion you choose. Because no religion teaches us to fight, quarrel or hurt anyone. But man gets his knowledge from people, those people who may not have read or understood those texts properly. That is why if you want to understand life, then read your scriptures yourself and try to understand what God wants to say to you. It will be as if there are rules of any game in today's world. If you don't know the rules then will you be able to play that game properly? No.

Now the question comes of which one scripture we should read or which religion should we accept. The answer is that you should read all the scriptures and understand all the religions. Just as the way to reach a destination may be different, everyone's destination is the same. Every religion teaches liberty, equality, and fraternity. Every religion says that whatever the religion in this world you follow, just make sure the deeds should be good. God is a tree, whose different branches have been given the form of religion. Every twig means that some leaves ie people come out of every religion. But every branch forgets that its root is the same, and its leaves are also the same. A person who understands this always achieves success in life.

This is the reason that only a few people are successful in the world because they have complete knowledge of their scriptures.

In this book, I have included some of the things that I have got from the Vedas, Puranas, Quran, Bible, and other religious texts. This book contains all that is common in all religions. This, along with making every human being a better person, makes man aware of the rules of this world.

Prologue

There are many such things in the Bhagavad Gita and the Bible of Jesus which are exactly the same. This is also because Buddha was born 623 years before Jesus was born and the teachings he taught reached the Greek community even before Jesus was born. Enlightenment in Buddhism reached through the Gita. Gautam Buddha followed the Gita and spread what he agreed, with as Buddhism to the rest of the world.

Whatever the religion, there is only one God. Therefore, the things told by God are also the same. Gautam Buddha was a great thinker and he spread the message of God in the world through his intuition.

The teachings given in Bhagavad Gita, Bible, and Quran, are related to spirituality not religion. But today's man in this world sees and understands all these teachings from the religious point of view instead of understanding them from the spiritual point of view. One has to awaken himself in the state of self-knowledge and understand that God is not attained by following religion but by following spirituality.

Now let me introduce you to some similarities, which are exactly the same in the Gita and the Bible.

In the seventh chapter of the Bhagavad Gita, it has been said by Shri Krishna that all the intelligent persons who are there, all love me and I love them. Similarly in the Bible, it is said by Jesus (John XIV. 21), that the one who loves me will be loved by both me and my Father.

In the ninth chapter of Bhagavad Gita, it has been said by Shri Krishna that I am the guide, supporter, master, abode, refuge and friend of human. Similarly in the Bible, it is said by Jesus (John XIV. 6), that I am the way of life for human and I am the truth. I am the beginning of man and I am the end.

In the sixth chapter of Bhagavad Gita, it has been said by Shri Krishna that nothing in this world can ever be separated from me and neither can I be separated from them. Similarly in the Bible, it is said by Jesus (John VI. 57), that the whole world resides in me and I reside in the whole world.

It is also said by Shri Krishna in the sixth chapter of the Bhagavad Gita that those who worship me with true devotion and love, they always reside in me and I in them. Similarly in the Bible, it is said by Jesus (John XVII 23), that I can be perfected in human and human in me.

In the ninth chapter of Bhagavad Gita, it has also been said by Shri Krishna that a person who worships me with true devotion, never faces any calamity. Similarly it is said by Jesus in the Bible, (John III. 5), that whoever believes in me will never punished and live a happy life.

In the tenth chapter of the Bhagavad Gita, it has been said by Shri Krishna that I am the beginning, middle and end of all living entities, non-living things. Similarly as said by Jesus in the Bible, (Rev. I. 8), I am the beginning, middle and end of all.

In the eighteenth chapter of the Bhagavad Gita, it has been said by Shri Krishna, O man! I will deliver you from all sins, why do you worry? Similarly it is said by Jesus in the Bible, (Matt. IX. 2), that son, you'll be happy forever, all your sins will be forgiven.

In the ninth chapter of the Bhagavad Gita, it has been said by Shri Krishna that whatever sacrifice, charity, or penance performed without faith is never fruitful and it is inauspicious to do so. Similarly, it is said by Jesus in the Bible (Rom. XIV. 23), that whatever is done without faith is tantamount to sin.

ONE

ESSENCE OF ALL RELIGIONS

Every religion says that a man's experiences definitely save him from wrong decisions, but his experiences come only from wrong decisions.

♡♡♡

Every religion says that the most expensive thing in a man's life is peace.

♡♡♡

Every religion says that any living being on this earth, its tears come out only when there is a lot of pain in its heart.

♡♡♡

Every religion says that the best friend in a man's life is his confidence.

ᑭᑭᑭ

Every religion says that a man should understand with an example of a needle how he walks on the cloth and sews it because it is not necessary that every prickly thing has a bad purpose.

ᑭᑭᑭ

Every religion says that a man should keep in mind that he should not focus on someone calling him good, but try to focus on that person who calls him bad.

ᑭᑭᑭ

Every religion says that in human life, man should remember that as long as he has faith in God, till then there will always be a way in his every confusion.

ᑭᑭᑭ

Every religion says that one should remember that if a sick person is to be cured, then cook khichdi in a vessel, because if you cook khichdi in the mind, it will make a person sick.

ঢঢঢ

Every religion says that one should always remain calm, no matter what one says, because no matter how strong the sun may be, it can never dry the sea.

ঢঢঢ

Every religion says that in human life a person can win or lose in human life, but it is difficult to beat the one who wins the hearts of others.

ঢঢঢ

Every religion says that if a man wants to reduce the difficulties of his life, then he has to understand the difference between his needs and desires.

ঢঢঢ

Every religion says that in this world it is very difficult to defeat a person who has learned to walk by stumbling blocks.

ঢঢঢ

Every religion says that the most valuable thing for a man in this world is sleep, peace, air and breath. And he gets it for free, yet he doesn't appreciate it.

Every religion says that in this world what things a man has to ignore in his life, if he knows this, then no one can stop him from being successful.

Every religion says that in this world the person who is not afraid of his future, only that person can enjoy the best of his present.

Every religion says that if a person in this world makes himself good instead of looking for good people, then perhaps the search for someone else will be completed by meeting him.

Every religion says that only man in this world is young and keeps on learning, even if he is old. And every person is old who stops learning, even if he is young. A man should always keep his mind young in his life.

Every religion says that the most difficult task for a man in this world is to assess himself, he should keep trying continuously to pass himself in self-improvement.

❦❦❦

Every religion says that if a man wants to be happy in this world, then he has to reduce his grievances. Otherwise the more complaints there are, the more unhappy he will be.

❦❦❦

Every religion says that in human life one should not be proud of his fame, because in his last time he needs someone's support.

❦❦❦

Every religion says that in human life it is very important to understand that the work obtained by recognition lasts only for a short time, but the identity obtained by work lasts for a lifetime.

❦❦❦

Every religion says that in this world, for a man, his upbringing and his rites are very important, just by reading and writing, one does not become a human.

***

Every religion says that in the life of a man in this world, likewise, a person does not have to do bad deeds, they get done by him, and in the same way, good deeds are not done automatically but man has to do it himself.

***

Every religion says that in this world man can reach heights only by thinking of change, through vengeance he only creates obstacles for himself.

***

Every religion says that one should remember that only those desires are good, in which there is no need to pledge self-respect.

***

Every religion says that one should believe that the decisions made by God are better than the wishes of every human being.

***

Every religion says that if a person wants to understand life, then he has to look back i.e. in the

past and if he wants to live life then he has to look forward i.e. towards his future.

ÞÞÞ

Every religion says that a person should keep this in mind in his life, that just as the winds change the course of the weather, in the same way, prayers change the attitude of trouble.

ÞÞÞ

Every religion says that a man should keep this in mind in his life, that the life he got is a matter of luck, his death is a matter of time, but even after death, it is a matter of deeds to remain alive in the hearts of people.

ÞÞÞ

Every religion says that a man's life begins to end from the day humans keep silence on the issues that matter to their life.

ÞÞÞ

Every religion says that one should be patient in life because the time comes for everyone. Just as the calendar always changes the date, one day such a date also comes, which changes that calendar itself.

ꝑꝑꝑ

Every religion says that in human life, even if the loud voice of a false person silences the true person, the silence of the true person always shakes the roots of the false person.

ꝑꝑꝑ

Every religion says that it is not wrong for a man to lose in the world, but it is wrong to give up.

ꝑꝑꝑ

Every religion says that human behavior should be like a needle, not like a scissor, because the needle works to unite 2, and the scissor works to cut 1 into 2.

ꝑꝑꝑ

Every religion says that one should always remember that as you have friends, so will your future, that is why choose friends wisely.

ꝑꝑꝑ

Every religion says that one should always remember not to misuse time because even time does not have enough time to give time to anyone again.

ꕤꕤꕤ

Every religion says that if a person understands his own human life, then there is joy in his life alone, and if he does not understand then he is all alone throughout his life.

ꕤꕤꕤ

Every religion says that if a man speaks through his mind, then decisions are made, but if he keeps them in mind, then there are differences.

ꕤꕤꕤ

Every religion says that man should learn to forgive because he himself expects this from his God.

ꕤꕤꕤ

Every religion says that the relationship of human beings is not deepened by talking about big things, but by understanding small feelings. The cost of a mirror may be less than a diamond, but after wearing diamond jewelry, everyone looks for a mirror only.

ꕤꕤꕤ

Every religion says that in this world man is defeated only because he stops walking, but time works in the opposite. Because whether it is sun or shade, black night or rain, no matter how bad the situation, time always goes on. That's why time wins, if a man also keeps on moving like time, then he too will never lose.

♡♡♡

Every religion says that when time takes a turn in the life of any human being in this world, it not only turns the stakes but also changes the whole life of that person.

♡♡♡

Every religion says that no man can be happy in this world unless it is more important in his life to look happy than to be happy.

♡♡♡

Every religion says that the best friend of a person in this world is his conscience, who praises good deeds and shakes him up on bad deeds.

♡♡♡

Every religion says that in this world it is necessary for a person to know what is most important for him

in his life? If a man knows this, then he can achieve those things even in difficult situations.

♡♡♡

Every religion says that man keeps on moving around in his life with a bundle of karma, that is how he fills it through his own deeds and this is also the law of life.

♡♡♡

Every religion says that if human beings are not excited about any goal as soon as they wake up in the morning, then that human being is not living, only taking life.

♡♡♡

Every religion says that in this world a man should remember that no matter how difficult he finds his life, he can always do something and be successful in it.

♡♡♡

Every religion says that in this world man should always keep his eyes on what he wants to get, but man does the opposite, he keeps his eyes on what he has lost.

ÞÞÞ

Every religion says that in this world man should live his life according to the choice of God because in this world people's choices and people themself keep on changing.

ÞÞÞ

Every religion says that in this world if a man fights for his life by making God a justice, then victory will always be his.

ÞÞÞ

Every religion says that in this world man should never give up hope from God and should never expect from the world.

ÞÞÞ

Every religion says that after imagining a man in this world, he should also implement it, nothing will be achieved just by looking at the stairs, until you climb them.

ÞÞÞ

Every religion says that if a man wants peace in this world, then he can get it only through himself, only

through others will get entangled.

ÞÞÞ

Every religion says that in this world if a person should give these three gifts i.e. helping someone along with time and dedication, then he should never leave the company of such a person.

ÞÞÞ

Every religion says that every task in this world is difficult for every human being before it becomes easy for them.

ÞÞÞ

Every religion says that in this world man should remember that he should never pretend that he has no shortage of time.

ÞÞÞ

Every religion says that in this world a man may regret his speech, but he will never regret his silence.

ÞÞÞ

Every religion says that in this world only friendship can double man's happiness and half the sorrows.

Every religion says that if a person takes a lamp for others in this world, then the light will fall on him too and his face will also shine.

Every religion says that in this world where man's virtues uplift him, his sins snatch everything from him by slapping him.

Every religion says that in this world man should remember that if a lion sits on a rock, then that rock is also called a throne. Therefore, try to become a lion, not to get the throne, so wherever you sit, that place becomes your throne.

Every religion says that if a person in this world has a tendency to get a stone of his name printed or to get his name printed by giving a little donation, then he comes in the category of low category because it does not give charity or service, but to get praised. The sense of ego is hidden in this kind of work.

ᑭᑭᑭ

Every religion says that in this world, if a person starts considering dust as a color in the journey of his life, then it reflects that he has started understanding every move of his life.

ᑭᑭᑭ

Every religion says that in this world one human crosses the path of another man, cats are just infamous for crossing paths with humans.

ᑭᑭᑭ

Every religion says that if a man does not set rules for himself in this world, then he has to follow the rules made by others.

ᑭᑭᑭ

Every religion says that if any person in this world needs your advice, then give your advice along with your assistance because advice might go wrong, but

not the assistance.

ÞÞÞ

Every religion says that man should remember that as long as man is immersed in his ego, neither he will see his own faults nor the goodness of others.

ÞÞÞ

Every religion says that even if a human being does not speak, then his words can only be listened to by God. But, If God does not speak and yet a man listens, then he is a true devotee.

ÞÞÞ

Every religion says that in this human life, a man may forgive someone again and again, but a man should believe in another man only once.

ÞÞÞ

Every religion says that in this world man should keep doing good deeds because the good done towards anyone in life does not go in vain, only God knows when it will come back to you in what form.

ÞÞÞ

Every religion says that in this world the living beings who support each other never see the situation, and the people who see the situation never support anyone.

ÞÞÞ

Every religion says that if a man is not patient in this world, then he has neither present nor future.

ÞÞÞ

Every religion says that in this world a man should remember that time is not dumb, it just remains silent, and only when the right time comes, does it tell that it also knows how to speak.

ÞÞÞ

Every religion says that in this world it may be difficult for a man to read the world in the form of a book, but the world is the teacher who teaches him everything.

ÞÞÞ

Every religion says that if a person has more than what is needed in this world, then he should share it with those who need it more.

ÞÞÞ

Every religion says that it is the habit of every man in this world, if he does not get what he wants then he does not have patience and if he gets it then he does not appreciate it.

ꝑꝑꝑ

Every religion says that every human being in this world has to understand that if his goal in his life is big then his struggle will also be equally big.

ꝑꝑꝑ

Every religion says that even if a man is illiterate in this world, if he learns to understand the feelings of any creature, then he is the most educated man in the world.

ꝑꝑꝑ

Every religion says that when a person is on the path of struggle in this world, then he should not look back at that time, but after being successful he should not forget to look back.

ꝑꝑꝑ

Every religion says that man in this world has to remember that you are good to other human beings

as long as you fulfill their expectations, and all human beings are good to you as long as you are good to them. Don't have any hope.

ÞÞÞ

Every religion says that the value of earthen pots and family in human life is known only to the maker, not the destroyer.

ÞÞÞ

Every religion says that the definition of sin and virtue for human beings in this world is only that, the act which hurts one's heart is sin, and which brings laughter on one's face is a virtue.

ÞÞÞ

Every religion says that man should remember that problems in man's life do not come to ruin him, they come only to identify the self-power within that man.

ÞÞÞ

Every religion says that man must fight for his rights in this world, but he should not be tempted by whom he does not have rights.

ÞÞÞ

Every religion says that in this world a person who does not have the knowledge of the right direction and right time, even the rising sun is seen setting.

ꝒꝒꝒ

Every religion says that where a man is not present in this world, his merits and demerits represent him.

ꝒꝒꝒ

Every religion says that in this world a man should remember that no matter how proud the sea may be, it can drown the whole world, but a small drop of oil can cross that whole sea comfortably.

ꝒꝒꝒ

Every religion says that in this world man will find lakhs of excuses to be scattered, but he himself will have to find opportunities to join in his life.

ꝒꝒꝒ

Every religion says that in this world God sends a man with so much certainty. He doesn't have to bring anything when he is born, and he takes nothing with him when he is dead.

ꝒꝒꝒ

Every religion says that with the age of man in this world, his eyesight may become weak, but with time he starts seeing a lot clearer.

♡♡♡

Every religion says that no creature in this world should treat another creature in a way that it does not like for itself.

♡♡♡

Every religion says that in this world man should remember that no matter how weak the mirror is, he is never afraid to show the truth.

♡♡♡

Every religion says that in this world, one should remember that the sweetness in the relationship starts from the moment when both of them see fewer qualities and more flaws in each other.

♡♡♡

Every religion says that if a person is fond of finding evil in this world, then it is better that he starts it with himself and not with others.

ƤƤƤ

Every religion says that there are only two personalities of man in this world, which enhance him. The first when you have nothing is 'endurance' and the second when you have everything then 'behavior'.

ƤƤƤ

Every religion says that in this world man should remember that time never stops, if yesterday was bad then today good will also come.

ƤƤƤ

Every religion says that in this world man should keep the truth to himself, love others and have compassion for all, this is the grammar of life.

ƤƤƤ

Every religion says that in this world man should understand the power of words, that if it can make a relationship with someone then it can also spoil it.

ƤƤƤ

Every religion says that man should remember that hope and faith are never wrong in this world, but it

depends on us, whom we hoped and believed.

♡♡♡

Every religion says that man should remember that the highest interest in this world comes from investing capital in knowledge. He should always try to write something that is worth reading or do something that is worth writing about.

♡♡♡

Every religion says that in this world a man should learn to trust God like a child, just as if he throws that child in the air, he laughs, does not fear... because he knows that the one who loves him will never let him fall.

♡♡♡

Every religion says that good people have a specialty in human life, they are good even in bad times.

♡♡♡

Every religion says that man should remember that even though there may be more than one heir to any man's property on earth, he himself is the heir to the deeds done by him.

♡♡♡

Every religion says that man should remember that man's wealth is neither wealth nor property, his wealth is his smiling family, good health, well wishing, and his own contented mind.

⚐⚐⚐

Every religion says that one should always learn from life that even silence does good deeds as everyone must have seen trees that give shade to others.

⚐⚐⚐

Every religion says that one should remember never show the power of your tongue to those who have taught you to speak.

⚐⚐⚐

Every religion says that if someone digs a pit in your path in this world, do not be upset, because these are the people from whose presence you will learn to jump.

⚐⚐⚐

Every religion says that in human life in this world, meaning is very heavy because after leaving it

lightens every relationship.

♡♡♡

Every religion says that if someone in this world asks why God is not visible? So to say - only god is there when no one is there for you.

♡♡♡

Every religion says that some human beings in this world often feel that the life of others is better than theirs, but while assessing they forget that they are also others for them.

♡♡♡

Every religion says that in this world man should remember that ego is the opposite of knowledge, more knowledge, less ego.

♡♡♡

Every religion says that in this world man should keep assessing himself from time to time whether it is not whether kindness, compassion, humanity, friendship, practicality or humanity is decreasing or increasing.

♡♡♡

Every religion says that while making relationships in this world, it should be kept in mind that even though it is very easy to make relationships, it is very difficult to maintain them.

♡♡♡

Every religion says that in this world, one should remember that it is better to remain silent until one is fully aware of everything because incomplete truth is many times more dangerous than complete falsehood.

♡♡♡

Every religion says that in this world a person should remember that he cannot harm that person by being jealous of anyone, but he can definitely ruin his sleep and happiness.

♡♡♡

Every religion says that in this world a man should always understand that, if he learns something from his mistakes, then those mistakes are a ladder for him, but if he does not learn, then mistakes are like an ocean for him. The decision is yours, whether to climb or sink.

♡♡♡

Every religion says that the day a man in this world will believe that everything is done according to the will of God. From that day onwards all his troubles will automatically end.

ᑭᑭᑭ

Every religion says that in this world man should remember how right he is and how wrong he is in this life, only two people know this, God and conscience.

ᑭᑭᑭ

Every religion says that in this world if a man has a complaint with anyone, then he has to talk to him, if you have a complaint with most the people, he has to talk to himself.

ᑭᑭᑭ

Every religion says that many times in the life of a man in this world, he gets out of the biggest troubles as if someone is supporting him, the name of this invisible power is God.

ᑭᑭᑭ

Every religion says that in this world, one should remember that no one rises suddenly, the sun also

rises slowly and rises, the one who has the ability of patience and penance, he illuminates the world.

ÞÞÞ

Every religion says that in this world man should remember that, karma has neither paper nor book, yet the whole world is accounted for.

ÞÞÞ

They ask - is there really Ram Setu? I said - Oh naive, the truth is that you are from Ram.

ÞÞÞ

Every religion says that human life is like a drop in this world, but human ego is bigger than the ocean.

ÞÞÞ

Every religion says that in this world a man should remember that, just as no one can spoil iron, but his own rust spoils it, similarly man has no one else but his own bad thoughts ruins him.

ÞÞÞ

Every religion says that in this world man should remember that he definitely gets time to change his

life, but he does not get life again to change the time.

ppp

Every religion says that in this world man should always remain calm, only by staying calm he will be able to strengthen his life because iron remains strong only when it is cold, not when it is hot.

ppp

Every religion says that if you feel happy in this world without any reason, then believe me, someone, somewhere, is praying to God for you.

ppp

Every religion says that it is almost impossible for a man to be empty in this world without bowing down, and if one wants to be free from ego, then bowing down is the only solution.

ppp

Every religion says that the wisest in this world is the one who learns the most. Powerful is the one who has control over his desires. Respected is one who respects others. And rich is he who is happy with what is around him.

ppp

Every religion says that in this world man should purify his heart, not intellect, to maintain relationships, that is, tell the truth, speak clearly, say in front, if he is one, he will understand and if he is a stranger, then he will be released.

ᑭᑭᑭ

Every religion says that all the human beings in this world have come into this world like a rough stone, the only difference is that someone was broken by their loved ones, someone was carved by their loved ones.

ᑭᑭᑭ

Every religion says that in this world man should remember that it is better to change the person in front than to take revenge.

ᑭᑭᑭ

Every religion says that in human life it is wise to praise from the heart, intervene with the mind and react with discretion... otherwise silence is better.

ᑭᑭᑭ

Every religion says that a man should remember that his prayers to God are never canceled...just, they are accepted at the best of times.

♡♡♡

Every religion says that man should make good the time he has got, if a person keeps looking for good times, then his whole life will be reduced.

♡♡♡

Every religion says that people in this world should forget the bitter thing and hold their hand, but people keep holding on to the matter and leave their hands.

♡♡♡

Every religion says that in this world, humans should remember that the person who walks on the path of struggle, he can change the world and the one who has won the battle through the nights, he can emerge as the sun.

♡♡♡

Every religion says that in human life, it is also necessary for every person to have some knowledge of chess because sometimes the front piece is moving and we keep on playing the relationship.

ÞÞÞ

Every religion says that if human beings have to make their dreams come true in human life, then they have to change their paths, not their principles. Because trees always change leaves, not roots.

ÞÞÞ

Every religion says that in human life, humans should understand that God cannot be everywhere, that's why they made mother and mother cannot be with us all the time, that's why God made sister.

ÞÞÞ

Every religion says that in human life, humans should find their success not in the lines of the hands, but in the sweat of the forehead.

ÞÞÞ

Every religion says that in human life, humans have to remember that, how many resources they have, it does not matter until they know how to use them.

♡♡♡

Every religion says that it is better in this world if humans keep their words in their mind and they should believe in doing more than speaking.

♡♡♡

Every religion says that if humans want to do something different in this world, then they have to walk away from the crowd because the crowd gives courage but takes away your identity from you.

♡♡♡

Every religion says that there are two best places in this world for human beings to live in this world, either in one's heart or in one's prayers.

♡♡♡

Every religion says that human beings in this world should always remember that God is God without you, but you are nothing without God.

♡♡♡

Every religion says that human beings in this world should always remember that nothing is available in this world without hard work, just as birds also have

to come out of their nests for grain.

ᑭᑭᑭ

Every religion says that in this world, human beings need their nature like a lamp, which gives as much light in the palace of the emperor as in the hut of a poor.

ᑭᑭᑭ

Every religion says that human beings in this world should understand that matches burn themselves before burning anything else, similarly the one who is angry destroys himself first and then others.

ᑭᑭᑭ

Every religion says that people in this world should remember that, if he is not wrong then never present himself in front of anyone, because the one who believes in you does not need explanation, and the one who does not believe in you He will not agree.

ᑭᑭᑭ

Every religion says that people in this world should remember that umbrella cannot stop the rain, but it definitely gives courage to stand in the rain. Similarly, self-confidence is not a measure of success, but it definitely gives the motivation to struggle.

ꕤꕤꕤ

Every religion says that in this world humans should treat their relationships and money equally because both are difficult to earn but very easy to lose.

ꕤꕤꕤ

Every religion says that in this world the peace of mind, good luck to be in control of the mind, bad luck to remember someone with the mind and if someone remembers with the mind that is the ultimate good fortune.

ꕤꕤꕤ

Every religion says that in the life of human beings, only one member of their family is enough to settle or destroy their house.

ꕤꕤꕤ

Every religion says that crematoriums in this world are full of ashes of people who thought that the world

could not go on without them.

ᑭᑭᑭ

Every religion says that no man in this world is defeated when he falls, he is defeated when he refuses to rise after falling.

ᑭᑭᑭ

Every religion says that the end of all human beings is the same in this world, what do humans do while they are alive, only this thing makes a human being different from another human being.

ᑭᑭᑭ

Every religion says that the way to live with respect for all human beings in this world is to become the person they claim to be.

ᑭᑭᑭ

Every religion says that power, money, hunger, greed, love, jealousy, ambition or pride, everything that is more than what is needed in life is poison for all human beings in this world.

ᑭᑭᑭ

Every religion says that in this world God resides in the houses where the parents laugh.

♡♡♡

Every religion says that in this world a man should forgive another man as you expects from god for yourself.

♡♡♡

Every religion says that if there will never be a bad time in the life of a man in this world, then he will never be able to know about the bad people hidden in his life.

♡♡♡

Every religion says that in this world, humans should always remember that either they have to learn to change with the times, or they will have to learn to change the times because nothing will happen by cursing the compulsions, if a man wants to move forward, then he should learn to walk anyway in any situation.

♡♡♡

Every religion says that there is no use in this world to spend the whole life in this, what other people say because in the end those people will just say, "Ram

Naam Satya Hai"

ÞÞÞ

Every religion says that in this world, human beings do not have to stay to collect flowers in their lives, move ahead, flowers will continue to bloom in your path.

ÞÞÞ

Every religion says that human beings are wonderful in this world, when they like something, they don't see evil... when they hate something, they don't see good.

ÞÞÞ

Every religion says that the world is full of good people in this world, if you are not meeting anyone then become a good human first.

ÞÞÞ

Every religion says that words are like a kind of food for human beings in this world. At what time, which word is to be served, the person who understands this is called a good cook.

ÞÞÞ

It is good that Lord Shri Ram had taken the monkey army to Lanka.. If he had taken humans, half of them would have been in favor of Ravana after seeing the golden Lanka.

ᚹᚹᚹ

Every religion says that in this world man only knows how much money he has, but he never knows how much time he has left. This is the biggest difference between money and time.

ᚹᚹᚹ

Every religion says that in this world a man cannot change the fate of anyone even if he wants, but can show him the way by giving him good inspiration, if given a chance, become someone's "charioteer", not "selfish".

ᚹᚹᚹ

Every religion says that in this world humans should learn to smile because life teaches crying as soon as one is born.

ᚹᚹᚹ

Every religion says that it does not matter to anyone in this world, whether you exist or not, You will be

treated as per your behaviour and need.

ÞÞÞ

Every religion says that in this world man can learn from Mahabharata that one's own understanding also matters, otherwise Arjuna and Duryodhana's gurus were the same.

ÞÞÞ

Every religion says that human beings should not compare their life with anyone else in this world because both the sun and the moon shine, but at their own time.

ÞÞÞ

Every religion says that people in this world should not waste their today thinking that I have many tomorrows.

ÞÞÞ

Every religion says that in this world human beings should understand that not every day can be good, but something good happens in every day.

ÞÞÞ

Every religion says that in this world human beings should understand that desires are only that good, in which there is no need to pledge self-respect.

♡♡♡

Every religion says that people in this world should understand that love is that string which is so strong that it can bind even God. But she does not bind herself in any bondage.

♡♡♡

Every religion says that in this world the support of loved ones is very necessary, if there is happiness then it increases and if there is sorrow then it gets divided.

♡♡♡

Every religion says that in this world humans should save only those memories which create a sparkle in the eyes..! Not those who cause wrinkles on the face.

♡♡♡

Every religion says that life is a colorful book for everyone in this world, the only difference is that someone is reading every page by heart, and someone is just turning pages.

ÞÞÞ

Every religion says that even if one's parents are illiterate in this world, but the ability to impart education and values is not in any school in the world.

ÞÞÞ

Every religion says that the whole game of life in this world is created by time, man only plays his role.

ÞÞÞ

Every religion says that half the beauty of human beings in this world is in their speech.

ÞÞÞ

Every religion says that in this world, whether the ray of sun or hope in the life of human beings, it removes all the darkness of life.

ÞÞÞ

Every religion says that both anger and storm are equal in this world, only after calming down, it is known how much damage has been done.

ᑭᑭᑭ

Every religion says that whatever is in the fate of a man in this world will come by running away but those who are not in luck will come and run away.

ᑭᑭᑭ

Every religion says that in this world man's eyes only give him vision but what he sees in others depends on his feelings.

ᑭᑭᑭ

Every religion says that in this world, humans should respect those who work and not those who fill their ears.

ᑭᑭᑭ

Every religion says that the one who loses in this world is the one who loses not from the world but from himself.

ᑭᑭᑭ

Every religion says that in this world humans should be courageous because it is the path which will take them to their destination. Have you ever heard that darkness has not allowed dawn?

ϸϸϸ

Every religion says that evil in this world, big or small, always causes destruction, because small or big hole in the boat sinks the boat.

ϸϸϸ

Every religion says that the possibility of dreams coming true in this world is the thing that makes human life interesting.

ϸϸϸ

Every religion says that in this world in human life, I am the best, it is self-confidence, but I am the best, it is ego. And the ego is the cause of its destruction.

ϸϸϸ

Every religion says that the past in this world is not with man, but he has the tomorrow to win.

ϸϸϸ

Every religion says that man must become big in this world but not in front of the one who has made you big.

♡♡♡

Every religion says that in this world, when the medicine goes into the body instead of the pocket, only then there is an effect, in the same way, life is successful if good thoughts enter the heart, not just by listening.

♡♡♡

Every religion says that if a person dares to speak the truth in this world, then God will surely give him the power to face the consequences.

♡♡♡

Every religion says that in this world, self-respect comes with self-reliance in the life of man.

♡♡♡

Every religion says that God does not keep paper or book in this world, yet he keeps the account of the whole world.

♡♡♡

Every religion says that in this world a man should remember that the greatest happiness in his life is in doing that work, which people say, that it is not for you.

❦❦❦

Every religion says that in this world man can win this world by his virtues, not by ego.

❦❦❦

Every religion says that in this world man gets everything in this world, only his mistake is not found.

❦❦❦

Every religion says that human beings in this world should learn to ignore those people who talk about you behind their back, because they deserve to be in that place, behind you.

❦❦❦

Every religion says that in this world human beings should remember that if they do anything wrong in life then they cannot attain heaven because the doors of heaven do not open for those who do wrong deeds.

***

Every religion says that the problem in Kali Yuga is not that the truth-tellers are decreasing, the problem is that the number of those who only listen to the truth of choice has increased.

***

Every religion says that in the life of any human being in this world, if friends, books, paths and thinking are wrong then they mislead, and if they are right they make life.

***

Every religion says that in this world there is no heaven greater than happiness in the life of any human being and there is no hell other than despair.

***

Every religion says that all the human beings in this world are so poor that even their breath is not their own, and the rich are so much that they own the god who is ruling all the three worlds.

***

Every religion says that all human beings in this world should remember that the tree of ego bears the fruit of destruction.

ᑭᑭᑭ

Every religion says that if the winds can change the course of the weather in human life, prayer can change the moments of trouble.

ᑭᑭᑭ

Every religion says that in this world, human beings should remember that they have to put their strength in their thoughts, not in their voice, because the harvest is done by rain, not by flood.

ᑭᑭᑭ

Every religion says that ego is such a race in the life of every living being in this world where every winner loses.

ᑭᑭᑭ

Every religion says that in this world human beings should not become good just for appearances because God knows you not from outside but from inside.

ᑭᑭᑭ

Every religion says that all human beings in this world have to write their own destiny because this is not a letter, which can be written by others.

ꟼꟼꟼ

Every religion says that there is no disease in this world greater than fear, and no medicine greater than courage.

ꟼꟼꟼ

Every religion says that in this world, the habit of sleeping for five minutes not only makes them sleep for hours, but this laziness life makes them many years behind.

ꟼꟼꟼ

Every religion says that in this world the those people are appreciated who deserves to be appreciated by others.

ꟼꟼꟼ

Every religion says that in this world suffering comes in the life of a human being so that he can understand the importance of happiness.

ꟼꟼꟼ

Every religion says that the basis of excellence in this world does not depend on sitting on a high seat but on high thinking.

♡♡♡

Every religion says that in this world, human beings have to understand that, if he has faith in his destiny, he will get what is written in his destiny, and if he has faith in himself, he will write whatever he wants.

♡♡♡

Every religion says that in this world, human beings do not need weather in order to do something in life, all the means will be gathered, they only need the determination.

♡♡♡

Every religion says that the habit of never giving up in this world can be transformed into the habit of winning every day.

♡♡♡

Every religion says that in this world, humans should keep in mind that if their time is bad then

they should work hard and when the time is good then they should help someone.

ᕈᕈᕈ

Every religion says that in this world God has sent all human beings like a blank page on earth, on the basis of qualities and qualifications, we have to fill our own price in it.

ᕈᕈᕈ

Every religion says that it is not necessary to be great to start in this world, but to be great a beginning is necessary.

ᕈᕈᕈ

Every religion says that a habit of time is very good in human life, that it changes.

ᕈᕈᕈ

Every religion says that in this world if a person keeps small things in his heart, then he will weaken his big relationships too.

ᕈᕈᕈ

Every religion says that no matter how wisely any person uses his words in this world, yet the listener understands and derives its meaning according to his ability and thoughts of the mind.

ℙℙℙ

Every religion says that a prayer full of faith made by any human in this world has the power to break all the shackles of darkness.

ℙℙℙ

Every religion says that in this world a man should have the belief that he should not just let himself be defeated, if he succeeds in doing this then no one can defeat him.

ℙℙℙ

Every religion says that the secret of change in human life in this world is that you should not put all your energy in fighting the old, but in creating the new.

ℙℙℙ

Every religion says that in this world, if someone doubts your good deeds in human life, then it does not matter, because the doubt is always on the purity of gold, not on the soot of coal.

♡♡♡

Every religion says that in this world, what in defeat, what in victory, I am not afraid in the slightest, whatever I get on the path of struggle, that is also right.

♡♡♡

Every religion says that in this world a person should remember that the one who is taking the test again and again, he will also give happiness when the time comes.

♡♡♡

Every religion says that in this world two horses run in the mind of man, one of evil and the other of good, the one to whom man keeps on giving more food, that wins.

♡♡♡

Every religion says that if ever in this world do it for others, then there will be no need to do it for yourself.

ꕤꕤꕤ

Every religion says that having a relationship in this world does not make a relationship, but keeping a relationship builds a relationship.

ꕤꕤꕤ

Every religion says that it is not easy for human beings to find happiness within themselves in this world, and it is not possible to find it anywhere else.

ꕤꕤꕤ

Every religion says that save your mind from being Kaikeyi (a character in RAMAYANA) in this world because when the mind becomes Kaikeyi, then some mantra(a character in RAMAYANA) is definitely available to fill the ear.

ꕤꕤꕤ

Every religion says that in this world man can make medicine for every disease of his body, but until he does not make any medicine for the bitterness of his tongue, his problems will not end.

ꕤꕤꕤ

Every religion says that in this world a lamp of 'soil' fights with the darkness all night, you are a lamp of 'God', what are you afraid of.

ᑭᑭᑭ

Every religion says that don't stay in this world only with those who make you happy, spend some time also with those who are happy to see you.

ᑭᑭᑭ

Every religion says that in this world 'roof' should not be proud of being 'roof' because as soon as one more floor is built on it, then 'roof' will become floor.

ᑭᑭᑭ

Every religion says that in this world some man fears that God is watching and some believe that God is watching.

ᑭᑭᑭ

Every religion says that in this world birds never give nests for the future of their children, they just teach them the art of flying.

ᑭᑭᑭ

Every religion says that tolerance in this world is not a sign of weakness, but a sign of strength, just as Lord Shri Ram had given proof of his strength by pleading for the ocean for three days.

ppp

Every religion says that in this world man can fight with the world but not with his loved ones, because to live with his loved ones, is not to win.

ppp

Every religion says that what are the words in this world, if the smell is attached, and if it is lost, then the wound.

ppp

Every religion says that in this world it takes a minute to make fun of relationships but we forget that life is decorated with relationships.

ppp

Every religion says that in this world God creates everyone from the same soil, the only difference is that someone is beautiful from "outside".. and someone from "inside".

ppp

Every religion says that there is a difference in the feet walking in this world, one in front and one behind, but neither the one ahead is proud nor the one behind is insulted because they know that after some time this situation is about to change in me, this is called life.

Every religion says that when time judges in human life, then witnesses are not needed.

Every religion says that when human beings earn money in this world, things come in the house, but when they earn someone's blessings, with wealth comes happiness, health and love.

Every religion says that no matter how much praise is given in this world, but insult should be done very carefully, because insult is a debt, which everyone pays with interest when given opportunity.

Every religion says that man is a misguided deity in this world, if he can walk in the right direction then no one is better than him.

♡♡♡

Every religion says that even storms are defeated in this world, where the boats are stubborn.

♡♡♡

Every religion says that the best sight in this world is the one who can see his shortcomings, because you wake up externally every day from your sleep, but you wake up internally that's a rare scenario.

♡♡♡

Every religion says that in this world if the stitching of relationships is done by feelings then it is difficult to break and if it is done by selfishness then it is difficult to survive.

♡♡♡

Every religion says that people in this world should listen to the advice of everyone, but should do that only for which your courage and conscience should support.

♡♡♡

Every religion says that if human beings have to move ahead in life in this world, then ego, greed, anger and fear have to be thrown in the dustbin.

♡♡♡

Every religion says that in this world, if a person learns to remain calm in life, then he will find himself very strong, because iron remains strong only when it is cold,but it can be molded into any shape when it is hot.

♡♡♡

Every religion says that ego is the root cause of all the big mistakes in the life of man in this world.

♡♡♡

Every religion says that in this world, all human beings are faster than their speed, but no one has been able to get ahead of their time and luck.

♡♡♡

Every religion says that in this world, education and rites are the basic mantra of living life in human life, education will never let you down and culture will never let you fall.

ÞÞÞ

Every religion says that in human life the praise given by the opponent is the best fame.

ÞÞÞ

Every religion says that it is our good fortune to have good people in this world and it is our ability to take care of them.

ÞÞÞ

Every religion says that in this world, humans should keep their heart like the ocean, only then the rivers will come to meet themselves.

ÞÞÞ

Every religion says that in this world the person who has beautiful thinking of his mind finds the whole world beautiful.

ÞÞÞ

Every religion says that in this world if a man sets a time limit for dreams, then that becomes his goal.

***

Every religion says that if human beings have the courage to accept and the determination to improve in this world, then a person can learn a lot.

***

Every religion says that no human life is easy in this world, but he can make it easy, some with style and some by ignorance.

***

Every religion says that the most profitable deal for any human being in this world is to sit with the elders because in a few moments they give you years of experience.

***

Every religion says that the lucky ones in this world are those who get ’time‘ and ’understanding‘ together, because often ’time’ does not have ‘understanding’, and when ‘understanding’ comes then ’time' gets out of hand.

***

Every religion says that if you keep on laughing in this world, then the world is with you, otherwise tears do not even find a place in your eyes.

ÞÞÞ

Every religion says that struggle in the life of all human beings in this world is the invitation of nature, the one who accepts it moves forward.

ÞÞÞ

Every religion says that there is only heart in this world, which works without rest, so keep it happy, whether it is yours or your loved ones.

ÞÞÞ

Every religion says that in this world do not get entangled in the search whether there is a God or not, keep the search whether we ourselves are human or not.

ÞÞÞ

Every religion says that seven generations experience what is fortunately received in this world. Seven generations suffer what is achieved through dishonesty.

ℙℙℙ

Every religion says that only hope in human life is such an energy that any darkness of life can be illuminated.

ℙℙℙ

Every religion says that in human life time is the only king, a person just acts like a king.

ℙℙℙ

Every religion says that in this world, humans should learn to speak sweetly, to bow down, to be most loving.

ℙℙℙ

Every religion says that pride does not belong to anyone in this world, even before breaking, the piggy bank feels that all the money belongs to him.

ℙℙℙ

Every religion says that if a snake is seen at home in this world, then people beat it with sticks and if it is seen on Shivling, then they give milk. People respect your position and place, not you.

ᑭᑭᑭ

Every religion says that power and money are the fruits of life in this world, family and friends are the root of life.

ᑭᑭᑭ

Every religion says that in this world, people should remember that what can be given from the heart is not with the hands.

ᑭᑭᑭ

Every religion says that in this world any human being should be the reason for someone's smile or not, but he should never be the reason for anyone's pain.

ᑭᑭᑭ

Every religion says that the name and identity of any human being in this world may be small, but it should be of itself.

ᑭᑭᑭ

Every religion says that why it happens in this world that people leave relationships but do not give up stubbornness.

♡♡♡

Every religion says that the tongue of any human being never slips in this world, always remember. Whatever is going on in the brain, it comes on the tongue.

♡♡♡

Every religion says that if human beings want wonderful relationships in this world, then follow them deeply, wonderful pearls are never found on the shore.

♡♡♡

Every religion says that in this world people run away from the mud so that the clothes do not get spoiled, that is why the mud gets false pride that people are afraid of it.

♡♡♡

Every religion says that there are many deals in the life of human beings in this world, but those who sell

happiness and those who buy sorrow are not found.

ÞÞÞ

Every religion says that trust in this world but don't sit on anyone's trust.

ÞÞÞ

Every religion says that the bad news for human beings in this world is that time flies, the good news is that you are its driver.

ÞÞÞ

Every religion says that it is good for human beings to be beautiful in this world but it is more beautiful to be good.

ÞÞÞ

Every religion says that in the journey of life of human beings in this world it often happens that the decision which is difficult is better.

ÞÞÞ

Every religion says that life of human beings is very short in this world, live it with laughter as much as possible, because memories come back, not time.

ᑭᑭᑭ

Every religion says that the distance between possible and impossible in this world depends on the determination of the person.

ᑭᑭᑭ

Every religion says that in this world, human beings get excuses by thinking about the problem, thinking about the solution gives way.

ᑭᑭᑭ

Every religion says that in this world the person who is never familiar with the struggle, history is witness for those kind of people, they never gets famous.

ᑭᑭᑭ

Every religion says that in this world man should always try to avoid small mistakes because man stumbles not from mountains but with stones.

ᑭᑭᑭ

Every religion says that in this world, what is in the mind of man should be clearly stated because in this world decisions are made by telling the truth and by telling lies there are distances.

ℙℙℙ

Every religion says that some human beings have this ability in this world, no matter how good you say, they find evil in it, so take care of yourself.

ℙℙℙ

Every religion says that hope never leaves anyone in this world, only people leave it in a hurry.

ℙℙℙ

Every religion says that in this world the crowd always walks on the path which seems easy, but it does not mean that the crowd always walks on the right path. Choose your own path, because no one knows you better than you.

ℙℙℙ

Every religion says that as long as we keep helping each other in this world, no one will fall whether it is business, family or society.

ℙℙℙ

Every religion says that all human beings in this world need to create a storm of their deeds, more than beating their heads at the door of fate, only by doing this the doors of fate will open.

ᑭᑭᑭ

Every religion says that in this world the world is won by words and mind, even today the heart is won by the heart itself.

ᑭᑭᑭ

Every religion says that the luckiest person in this world is the one who has hunger with food, sleep with bed and religion with wealth.

ᑭᑭᑭ

Every religion says that when a person's mind is weak in human life, then his circumstances become a problem. When the mind is stable then situations become challenges and when the mind is strong then circumstances become opportunities.

ᑭᑭᑭ

Every religion says that in this world a person should always keep the effect of a lamp, that too

without seeing whose house was illuminated by it.

♡♡♡

Every religion says that in this world a person's care for another human being shows how much he cares for another person. Otherwise there is no scales to measure relationships.

♡♡♡

Every religion says that everyone needs respect in this world but people forget to give back.

♡♡♡

Every religion says that if you have to ask something from God in this world, then always pray for the fulfillment of your mother's dreams, you yourself will touch the heights of the sky.

♡♡♡

Every religion says that in this world someone is enough, and someone alone is enough.

♡♡♡

Every religion says that in this world, man should have faith in both God and time in his bad times,

because time turns coal into diamond and Lord ranks as king.

PPP

Every religion says that in this world a person should accept what he feels is good, and he should give up what he feels bad. Be it thought, deed, or man.

PPP

Every religion says that in this world man should be identified not with big people but with those who support him on time.

PPP

Every religion says that in this world a man should remember that when he is climbing the stairs of the heights, then he should behave very well with the people left behind, because while descending the same people will meet him again on the way.

PPP

Every religion says that in this world there are bigger parents than God, because God gives both happiness and sorrow but parents give only happiness.

ꟼꟼꟼ

Every religion says that if gifts are not given to a child by a man in this world, he will cry for a while, and if the sacraments are not given, then he will cry for the rest of his life.

ꟼꟼꟼ

Every religion says that who should keep an account in this world, how much was given to whom and who saved how much, so God applied simple mathematics and sent everyone empty handed and called empty handed.

ꟼꟼꟼ

Every religion says that in this world a wise man finds a way in his difficult time, and a weak person pretends.

ꟼꟼꟼ

Every religion says that the most difficult posture in this world is 'Assurance', the longest breath is 'Faith', the most difficult yoga is 'disconnection' and the best yoga is 'cooperation'.

ꟼꟼꟼ

Every religion says that in this world a person's 'getting down in your mind' and 'getting out of mind' depends only on your behaviour.

♡♡♡

Every religion says that man is a shop in this world, and the tongue is its lock, once the lock opens up, only then it is known whether the shop is of gold or of coal.

♡♡♡

Every religion says that there is nothing better for him in human life in this world than his today, because his tomorrow will never come and today will never go.

♡♡♡

Every religion says that in this world a person does not know how many days he has to stay in the shelter of the world, that is why win everyone's hearts, this is the jewel of life.

♡♡♡

Every religion says that in human life, after one of his dreams is shattered, seeing his second dream, this courage is called life.

ᑭᑭᑭ

Every religion says that in this world man should not compare his life with anyone. Just like there is no comparison between 'Sun' and 'Moon', they shines as per their defined timings.

ᑭᑭᑭ

Every religion says that in this world the wounds of a man's mouth heal the fastest, but the wounds of words spoken with the mouth heal the longest.

ᑭᑭᑭ

Every religion says that in this world, those who have to be their own, they themselves become 'own', they are not made 'own' by telling anyone.

ᑭᑭᑭ

Every religion says that one has to go far in this world just to know who is near.

ᑭᑭᑭ

Every religion says that in this world, the better the speech and thoughts of a man, the more success he will get.

ᑭᑭᑭ

Every religion says that in this world the people who are not able to beat you 'by running' in the race of life, they try to defeat you 'by breaking'.

ᑭᑭᑭ

Every religion says that in this world it is not wrong to bow down in relationships in human life because if seen, even the sun sets for the moon.

ᑭᑭᑭ

Every religion says that no one can close the path God has opened for you in this world.

ᑭᑭᑭ

Every religion says that the silence of a person in this world is not his weakness but his nobility, otherwise he who knows how to bear it, also knows how to say it.

ᑭᑭᑭ

Every religion says that no human being in this world is full of all qualities, so some shortcomings should be ignored and relationships should be maintained.

♡♡♡

Every religion says that there is no fixed definition of earning for human beings in this world because experience, relationships, respect and good friends are all forms of earning.

♡♡♡

Every religion says that it is not a big deal for humans to earn bread in this world, it is a big thing to eat bread with family.

♡♡♡

Every religion says that in this world, humans should keep the door of their house small, because the one who has bowed down, think that he is his own.

♡♡♡

Every religion says that in this world people leave you at the slightest thing, and God holds you with a little prayer.

♡♡♡

Every religion says that in this world man should remember that time changes all time. Just give some time to time.

ᑭᑭᑭ

Every religion says that it is better for human beings in this world than to regret later, try once with your life.

ᑭᑭᑭ

Every religion says that if human beings face difficulties in this world, then they should be avoided by saying - "Just tell the destination,though I have not reached yet, since there are difficulties, but remember I haven't stopped yet".

ᑭᑭᑭ

Every religion says that in this world human beings should keep knocking on the doors of each other's mind so that if the meetings do not sound right, they will keep on coming.

ᑭᑭᑭ

Every religion says that in this world a person learns to speak after 2 years of birth. But it takes a whole

lifetime to learn what to speak.

ÞÞÞ

Every religion says that time, faith and respect are such birds in this world..! Those who fly away do not come back.

ÞÞÞ

Every religion says that all human beings in this world dream in their sleep, but God wakes them up every day and gives them a chance to fulfill those dreams. That is why we should give thanks to God everyday.

ÞÞÞ

Every religion says that in this world, people should always remember that faith and honesty are invaluable heritage of human beings.

ÞÞÞ

Every religion says that when a person gets into trouble in this world, then he starts seeing Griha Dosha, Vastu Dosha, Pitra Dosha, Shani Dosha, Kaal Sarp Dosh, only his own fault is not visible.

ÞÞÞ

Every religion says that if you have happiness in your heart while helping others in this world, then that is service, everything else is pretend.

Every religion says that in this world man is created by his belief, as he thinks, so he becomes.

Every religion says that talent is of no importance in this world without will power.

Every religion says that no man in this world can see evil in attachment and he cannot see good in hatred.

Every religion says that one who has hope in this world does not lose even after losing.

Every religion says that in this world through which 'doubt' enters in the life of human beings, 'love' and 'faith' go out through the same door.

ঢঢঢ

Every religion says that the value of human beings in this world is in what they are, not in what they have.

ঢঢঢ

Every religion says that bad company for a human being in this world is like a coal which burns hands when it is hot and turns hands black when it is cold.

ঢঢঢ

Every religion says that every person in this world is better than any other person in some thing or the other and we should learn those things from him.

ঢঢঢ

Every religion says that the only ones who win in this world are those who hold on to hope in every situation.

ঢঢঢ

Every religion says that if a man wants to be successful in this world, then he should always keep this thing in mind that he should not rely on strangers because you have to walk on your own feet.

Every religion says that in this world you keep doing good like flowing water, evil will itself be washed away like garbage.

Every religion says that the greatest use of life in this world is to invest it in something that will remain hereafter.

Every religion says that in this world, along with fasting food, greed, greed, slander, lust, anger, bad thoughts should also be there.

Every religion says that when you carve yourself in this world, then the world searches for you.

Every religion says that in this world man should keep relationships like sandalwood so that even if the pieces are a thousand, the fragrance does not go away.

♡♡♡

Every religion says that in this world man should keep in mind that nothing will happen by just looking at the clock, but you will have to do what the clock does, keep going continuously.

♡♡♡

Every religion says that there can be no better friend in this world than God.

♡♡♡

Every religion says that if a man in this world decides with his heart what he has to do, then his mind will automatically devise ideas.

♡♡♡

Every religion says that there are only two things in this world, by giving which no one gets anything, one smile and the other prayer, the more you distribute them, the more you will get.

♡♡♡

Every religion says that as long as man lives with his fear in this world, he will not be able to live his dreams.

ṖṖṖ

Every religion says that in this world, one's simple nature is not his weakness, but the sanskars given by his parents.

ṖṖṖ

Every religion says that if someone is the most powerful in this world, then it is willpower. You can get everything in the world through this. If you want, you will find the way automatically.

ṖṖṖ

Every religion says that the time is the same for every human being in this world, if he wants to make gold in that time, either waste it by sleeping.

ṖṖṖ

Gave a wonderful taunt, in the temple today, God said - "You only come to ask, come to meet you sometime".

ᑭᑭᑭ

Every religion says that when the games of childhood are over in human life, then the games of luck start.

ᑭᑭᑭ

Every religion says that in this world a man should remember that his life can suddenly take a good turn from anywhere in his life, that is why man should never be disappointed.

ᑭᑭᑭ

Every religion says that in this world it is not necessary that what is your age, it is important that what age do you think.

ᑭᑭᑭ

Every religion says that in this world you should offer yourself to God, this is the best support. He who knows its support is always free from fear, worry and grief.

ᑭᑭᑭ

Every religion says that in this world fragrance is found automatically to those who cultivate flowers.

ꝒꝒꝒ

Every religion says that compare yourself with a quiet and humble person in this world, you will feel that your pride is definitely worth giving up.

ꝒꝒꝒ

Every religion says that in this world a man should remember that he has to make as much effort to become a noble person as he does to become beautiful.

ꝒꝒꝒ

Every religion says that in this world small thoughts are capable of bringing big changes in the life of man. Just like the door is smaller than the house, the lock is smaller than the door, the key is smaller than the lock... but a small key opens the whole house.

ꝒꝒꝒ

Every religion says that in this world a teacher is necessary in the life of a man, not the ego.

ꝒꝒꝒ

Every religion says that in this world the eyes also have to be opened for light, the darkness does not go away just because the sun comes out.

ﮎﮎﮎ

Every religion says that in this world, you will always hear from the mouths of successful people that - 'If the sunshine on the path to success was not there, then we would have fallen asleep'.

ﮎﮎﮎ

Every religion says that if a man starts giving in this world, these things will start coming in his life, respect as well as wealth.

ﮎﮎﮎ

Every religion says that if you want only a handful in this world then become Alexander, if you want the whole universe then become Kabir.

ﮎﮎﮎ

Every religion says that in this world, the creation of god seems differently to everyone, according to their vision.

ﮎﮎﮎ

Every religion says that in this world, human beings feet take them to the temple and their conduct take them to God.

ÞÞÞ

Every religion says that in this world the fruit of hard work and the solution of the problem is definitely available at the right time.

ÞÞÞ

Every religion says that the ’strength‘ of a person in this world can be estimated, but not his ’spirits’.

ÞÞÞ

Every religion says that only love has the power to bow down someone in this world, otherwise what was the need for Ramji to eat berries tasted by shabri.

ÞÞÞ

Every religion says that your goal in this world should be right because even termites do work day and night, but they do not create but destroy.

ÞÞÞ

Every religion says that always remember in this world that there is no destination where there is no way to reach.

ꟼꟼꟼ

Every religion says that the fire of revenge in this world burns others less and more itself, that is why the idea of not taking revenge on anyone but changing oneself is better.

ꟼꟼꟼ

Every religion says that in this world a person should always keep his words sweet so that even if he has to take it back, he does not feel bitter.

ꟼꟼꟼ

Every religion says that never let a man blame his luck in this world, have been born as a human being, if this is not luck then what else is.

ꟼꟼꟼ

Every religion says that it is not possible to achieve anything in this world without renunciation, because even to breathe, one has to exhale first.

ꟼꟼꟼ

Every religion says that sweet tongue, good habits, good behavior and good people are always respected in this world.

ᑭᑭᑭ

Every religion says that if your voice is high in this world, only a few people will listen, but if the talk is high, then many people will listen.

ᑭᑭᑭ

Every religion says that in this world, humans should give time to every relation in their life, do you know tomorrow we will have time and there is no relationship.

ᑭᑭᑭ

Every religion says that for longevity in this world, halve the dose, drink twice as much water, exercise three times, laugh four times, and meditate on God one hundred times.

ᑭᑭᑭ

Every religion says that in this world even a soil lamp fights with the darkness all night, then you are a gift from God, what are you afraid of.

ℙℙℙ

Every religion says that when man is filled with anger in this world, then its hell for him and when man is filled with compassion then heaven.

ℙℙℙ

Every religion says that if hard work becomes a habit in this world, then success becomes luck.

ℙℙℙ

Every religion says that this is the principle of successful relationships in this world, forget all those things which are meaningless.

ℙℙℙ

Every religion says that in this world the mistake of man is when he forgets God.

ℙℙℙ

Every religion says that the best cure for man's anxiety in this world is his trust in God.

ᑭᑭᑭ

Every religion says that in this world, if the relationship is in the heart, then it is not broken even by breaking, and if it is in the mind, then it is not connected even by connecting.

ᑭᑭᑭ

Every religion says that in this world, the advice of the loser, the experience of the winner and one's own intellect never allow a person to be defeated.

ᑭᑭᑭ

Every religion says that human life in this world is like a guitar, which if a person learns to play it properly, then there is joy in his life.

ᑭᑭᑭ

Every religion says that happiness in this world is the medicine which is not found in any market of the world but only within itself.

ᑭᑭᑭ

Every religion says that whenever the boat of human life gets stuck in the middle of this world, only the boat called God crosses it.

ᑭᑭᑭ

Every religion says that in this world, you should become rich with your mind and not with money, because even if there are golden urns in the temple, one has to bow down on the steps of the temple.

ᑭᑭᑭ

Every religion says that in this world it is very important for man to bow down from his mind, only by bowing his head one does not get blessings of God.

ᑭᑭᑭ

Every religion says that to change life in this world one has to fight, to make it easy, one has to understand.

ᑭᑭᑭ

Every religion says that in this world the king in the country, the teacher in the society and the father in the family are never ordinary, both creation and destruction are in their hands.

ᑭᑭᑭ

Every religion says that in this world a person can be arbitrary in doing his deeds, but not in their karma.

Every religion says that to be successful in this world, the desire for success should be greater than the fear of failure.

Every religion says that the one who suffers sorrow in this world can be happy later, but the one who gives sorrow can never be happy.

Every religion says that not everyone can become great in this world, but everyone can be better than where they are at the moment.

Every religion says that in this world man cannot see evil in attachment and he cannot see good in hatred.

Every religion says that if there is a desire for peace in this world, then first pacify the desire.

ஐஐஐ

Every religion says that in this world a man should not indulge in unaccounted-for laughs, but he should take care of what he has got.

ஐஐஐ

Every religion says that it is always beneficial for a person to wake up early in this world, whether it is from sleep, ego or fear.

ஐஐஐ

Every religion says that this often happens in connection with misunderstandings in this world, every brick thinks that the wall rests on it.

ஐஐஐ

Every religion says that keep helping people in this world, because there is a principle of nature, the well from which people keep drinking water never dries up.

ஐஐஐ

Every religion says that due to arrogance of man in this world, all the three wealth, glory and lineage are lost. If you don't believe then see, Ravana, Kauravas, Kansa.

Every religion says that life in this world is not what we got, life is what we make.

Every religion says that to make mistakes in this world is "nature", to believe is "culture", to improve is "progress".

Every religion says that the thread whose knots can be opened in this world, scissors should not be used on that thread.

Every religion says that in this world a person remembers all the things that are forgotten, that is why there is controversy in his life.

Every religion says that in this world, believe that there is no giant like Banyan and Peepal. But remember that even the basil growing in pots is no less than anyone.

ÞÞÞ

Every religion says that many people in this world have come up after recovering from sorrows in life. What is falling apart can rise again, just have courage. When sorrow comes in life, our patience is tested.

ÞÞÞ

Every religion says that only needs depend on money in this world, not happiness. There are many people who have a lot of money, but not a little happiness.

9 798887 720005

Printed by Libri Plureos GmbH in Hamburg,
Germany